THE TEDDY BEAR BOOK

GW00319321

THE
TEDDY BEAR
BOOK

EDITED BY SUSAN FEUER

ARIEL BOOKS

ANDREWS AND MCMEEL
KANSAS CITY

All photos are from the Carrousel Shop and Museum
of Chesaning, Michigan, and were taken by Mocny
Photo-AV, Saginaw, Michigan.

ISBN: 0-8362-1524-9

Library of Congress Catalog Card Number: 96-83375

ACKNOWLEDGMENT

Thank you to Terry and Doris Michaud for sharing their collection and putting so much time into this project.

Teddy bears are such well-loved toys that it is hard to believe they have been around for less than one hundred years. Playmates, security blankets, and pillows all in one, teddy bears are treasured by children—and adults—the world over. Only a parent's hug is more comforting to a young child than snuggling with a beloved teddy bear.

Surely the teddy bear would not be so popular if President Theodore "Teddy" Roosevelt hadn't been an avid hunter and sportsman. In November 1902, Roosevelt traveled to Mississippi to hunt bears. The trip wasn't successful; in fact, Roosevelt's only opportunity to shoot game occurred when his guides presented him with a young bear tied to a tree. Thinking it cruel and unsporting to shoot a trapped animal, Roosevelt went home empty-handed. News of the president's refusal reached a cartoonist, Clifford K. Berryman, who drew a caricature of Roosevelt and the bear.

Soon thereafter, Morris and Rose Michtom, who ran a Brooklyn, New York, stationery and candy store, displayed a bear in their window that Rose had made and labeled it

"Teddy's Bear." The little bear caught on, and Butler Brothers, a wholesale toy distributor, bought all the "Teddy's Bears" that the Michtoms could make. The Michtoms eventually founded the Ideal Novelty and Toy Company to mass-produce teddy bears.

While the Michtoms may have coined the phrase "Teddy's Bear," they were not the first to create a stuffed bear. In Germany, seamstress Margarete Steiff sold felt clothing and stuffed animals by mail order. Her nephew, Richard, joined her company as a toy designer and specialized in making bears. Soon, the company produced nothing but bears. The demand for teddy bears, as they had become known, came mostly from America, where Teddy Roosevelt was serving his second term as president. The years 1903–8 were known to the company's owners as the *Bärenjahre:* the bear years. In 1907 Steiff produced 975,000 bears, a company record, which still stands to this day.

From 1900 to 1969 teddy bears changed very little; small modifications were made to coverings and stuffings as new materials became available. Then, in 1969, the teddy bear world underwent a drastic change:

British actor Peter Bull wrote *The Teddy Bear Book*. Not a collector, Bull was simply a teddy bear enthusiast who had never lost his childhood love for teddy bears. In the 1970s and 1980s, bears became adult collectibles; they were no longer just children's toys. Teddy-mania had begun: teddy bear magazines were published, teddy bear shows were organized, teddy bear museums were founded, and conventions were held.

Another offshoot of teddy bear mania was teddy bear artists. These artists both design and produce limited editions of unique, handmade bears, which are greatly prized by collectors. The market for artist-made bears is an adult one; many of these bears are labeled "for adults only," because they often don't meet the safety standards required for toys.

The teddy bears in this book are all from the Carrousel Shop and Museum in Chesaning, Michigan, run by Terry and Doris Michaud. The Michauds not only collect bears—they have over four hundred—they also design and make them. These Michaud-designed teddies are produced and distributed by the Deans Company of Great Britain.

Internationally recognized experts in their field, the Michauds have written four teddy bear books and regularly contribute articles to teddy bear magazines in the United States and abroad. Their obsession with teddies can all be blamed on "The Professor," the first bear in their collection. According to Terry, "It's all his fault we started this."

10-INCH BEAR
STEIFF
GERMANY
1903

One of Steiff's first productions, this bear's mohair has all but worn away. Steiff re-issued a copy of this bear in 1984 to honor the Margaret Woodbury Strong Museum, Rochester, New York, a museum that has an extensive toy collection.

10-INCH BEAR
STEIFF
GERMANY
1904

An early Steiff bear, it has lost every bit of the mohair that originally covered it. While moths may have gotten its fur, the metal button that identifies the bear as a Steiff remains intact.

15-INCH BEAR
MANUFACTURER UNKNOWN
GERMANY
1904

Made of cinnamon-colored mohair, with black shoe-button eyes and long arms, this bear has a vaudeville background: it once belonged to a member of the Ziegfeld Follies. Because it has a funnel-shaped head, this teddy belongs to a group of bears known as "cone heads." Although the bear's body is torn in a few spots, its felt pads are in mint condition.

20-INCH BEAR
STEIFF
GERMANY
1907

A rare Steiff with a leather muzzle, this bear was originally purchased by the owner's father from the Butler Brothers Company in Minneapolis, a major toy distributor in the early twentieth century. The bear sat for forty years overseeing the goings-on at its owner's Mexico City restaurant.

12-INCH BEAR
STEIFF
GERMANY
1909

A thin but well-loved Steiff, this bear has a hole in its right ear where its trademark metal button once was.

20-INCH BEAR
STEIFF
GERMANY
1910

Nicknamed "The Old Man's Bear," this rare cinnamon-colored Steiff bear is made from long, curly mohair. It was acquired from its original owner—when he was in his eighties.

24-INCH BEAR
IDEAL
AMERICA
1910

Made from gold mohair, this large bear is a
good example of an early American teddy.

19-INCH BEAR
IDEAL
AMERICA
1915

Nicknamed "The Professor," this light gold mohair teddy is the first bear collected by Terry and Doris Michaud. When purchased, the bear was missing an ear, which has since been restored.

22-INCH BEAR
MANUFACTURER UNKNOWN
AMERICA
1915

Made from dark gold mohair, this large teddy bear is in excellent condition. Although the exact manufacturer is unknown, it is believed to be an early Ideal bear.

11-INCH TEDDY GIRL
SIMON & HALBIG
GERMANY
1918

Concerned that girls would shy away from dolls in favor of teddy bears, doll manufacturers came up with the teddy girl, a toy with a doll's head and a plush bear body. Unfortunately, their creation flopped. Since so few were produced, teddy girls are rare and highly prized by collectors.

5-INCH BABY RATTLE
STEIFF
GERMANY
1918

Made from white mohair and in excellent
condition, this bear conceals a baby rattle
inside its torso.

4 ½-INCH PERFUME BOTTLE BEAR
SCHUCO
GERMANY
1920s

One of the most sought-after teddy bears in the world, its head comes off to reveal a glass perfume bottle. This novelty bear is in mint condition.

14-INCH BEARS
MANUFACTURER AND
COUNTRY UNKNOWN
1920S

The knitted bear on the right was purchased by the Michauds in Great Britain. Months later, Doris Michaud, on a hunch, unraveled the knitting and found underneath it the antique teddy bear on the left. The original owner had knit a new body for the old and worn bear, and placed this new "coat" over the old.

19-INCH BEAR
PETZ COMPANY
GERMANY
1923

This well-loved bear was a childhood trea-
sure of a man who was killed in World War
II. "Tommy's Bear," as it is nicknamed, is
made from light beige mohair.

5-INCH MECHANICAL BEAR
SCHUCO
GERMANY
1930s

This is a rare mechanical dancing teddy, which, when it is wound, dances and spins on its metal feet.

4-INCH BEAR
STEIFF
GERMANY
1930s

Called Teddyli, this bear has a rubber body and mohair head. Wearing its original clothes, this teddy shows the variety of materials from which bears were made.

30-INCH BEAR
MANUFACTURER UNKNOWN
GREAT BRITAIN
1930s

Rare because few of its size were produced
in the 1930s, this English Winnie-the-Pooh
bear is appropriately honey colored.

22-INCH BEAR
KNICKERBOCKER
AMERICA
1930s

Made from cinnamon-colored mohair, this bear is nicknamed "The Storekeeper" because it spent most of its early years guarding a country store.

14-INCH MECHANICAL BEAR
SCHUCO
GERMANY
1932

Depending on which way you move its tail, this rare mechanical bear nods or shakes its head. Called a "yes/no" bear, it is dressed in its original costume, a bellhop uniform.

8-INCH BEAR
STEIFF
GERMANY
1935

Named "Bearkin," this teddy was produced by Steiff for F.A.O. Schwarz; it came with a trunk that held its extensive wardrobe. Made from white mohair, with a brown stitched nose and claws, Bearkin has an unusual feature: a red stitched mouth.

22-INCH BEAR
CHAD VALLEY
GREAT BRITAIN
1950s

Chad Valley, a British bear manufacturer, produced this light gold long-haired teddy in the 1950s. A label on its right foot reads, "By Appointment to H. M. Queen Elizabeth."

4 ½-INCH KOALA BEAR
STEIFF
GERMANY
1955

A non–teddy bear with a jointed head and felt hands, feet, and nose, this koala is made from beige mohair, the color of which closely resembles real koala fur.

11-INCH BEAR
HOUSE OF NISBETT
GREAT BRITAIN
1977

This dark brown mohair bear was made in honor of Queen Elizabeth's jubilee, the twenty-fifth anniversary of her 1952 coronation.

1 ¼-INCH BEAR
SARA PHILLIPS
MARYLAND
1980

This extraordinarily tiny bear (made of white felt) was handmade by Sara Phillips, as were the trunk, hat, and honey pot.

18-INCH CHRISTOPHER ROBIN DOLL
7-INCH WINNIE-THE-POOH BEAR
R. JOHN WRIGHT
AMERICA
MID-1980s

These well-known figures are from A. A. Milne's *Winnie-the-Pooh;* the character of Pooh was based upon Milne's son's teddy bear. This Pooh is a wool and mohair blend. Made of sculptured felt, the Christopher Robin doll is one of a limited edition of five hundred and is highly sought after by bear and doll collectors alike.

6-INCH BEAR
CANTERBURY BEARS
GREAT BRITAIN
1985

Signed by Maude and John Blackburn, the
couple that runs Canterbury Bears, this pale
gold mohair bear wears an English bobby
helmet.

4½-INCH BEAR
ROSEMARY JORDAN
AMERICA
1986

Rosemary Jordan created this little bear
from an antique quilt.

2¾-INCH BEAR
DICKIE HARRISON
MARYLAND
1988

Dickie Harrison crafted this miniature version of the Michaud's first bear, "The Professor," out of light gold upholstery fabric, a short-napped material.

17-INCH PAPER BAG BEAR
ANITA CROWELL
MICHIGAN
1990s

Artist Anita Crowell made this unique bear from paper grocery bags. This paper creation is a pun on "bag bears," which are unjointed bears made from a single piece of fabric.

2¾-INCH BEAR
SHIRLEY HOWEY
ARIZONA
1990s

Nicknamed "Woody," this bear was created out of upholstery fabric that looks like wood.

2¼-INCH BEAR
SHIRLEY HOWEY
ARIZONA
1990s

This colorful, tiny bear is made from upholstery fabric that is patterned to resemble stained glass.

2¼-INCH BEAR
ARTIST UNKNOWN
AUSTRALIA
1990

Made of felt, this miniature version of a
Winnie-the-Pooh bear was handcrafted by
residents of an Australian nursing home, as
a fund-raiser for the facility.

12-INCH BEAR
8-INCH BEAR
STEIFF
GERMANY
1992 AND 1995

An Alfonzo bear and a baby Alfonzo bear, these are limited editions produced by Steiff for Teddy Bears of Witney, a shop in England. The original Alfonzo, made in 1908, was commissioned by the Grand Duke of Russia for his daughter, who brought the bear with her when she visited Buckingham Palace in 1914.

The text of this book is set in Bembo and
the display in Copperplate Gothic by
Snap-Haus Graphics in Edgewater, N.J.

Line art by Robyn Officer

Book design by Diane Stevenson of
Snap-Haus Graphics